DISABILITY EMPOWERMENT

FREE MONEY FOR DISABLED AMERICANS TO MAKE DREAMS REALITY

By Tonza Borden

Published by
LuLu Enterprises
860 Aviation Parkway
Suite 300
Morrisville, NC 27560

Published by LuLu Enterprises
860 Aviation Parkway
Suite 300
Morrisville, NC 27560

Visit our Web site at www.lulu.com

Printed in the United States of America

ISBN: 978-1-4303-2888-9

Book Design by LuLu.com

DISCLAIMER

This information is distributed with the understanding that the author and publisher are not engaged in rendering legal, accounting, or other professional advice. If legal advice or other expert assistance is required, the services of a competent professional should be sought. Also note that this information in no way guarantees any specific amount of money to be obtained and the author and publisher can not be held responsible for any actions that you may take. The samples and information that Tonza Borden shares with you in this book are the result of her experience in obtaining services. They represent her best knowledge of workable methods.

There is no way to guarantee that the information will apply to your particular type of application. However, the information that follows does have a proven track record and is supplied to provide you with guidance. It is the user's sole responsibility to determine the applicability of the material to his or her use, and the author and publisher assume no responsibility for situations which may arise from the user's application of this material to his or her own situation. Sales that are printed, spiral-bound and shipped through the postal service by Tonza Borden (instead of downloading or purchasing a trade paperback) are done so by special customer request and are non-refundable.

There is no God but Jehovah.

A DISABLED MANIFESTO

We proclaim that we are born free and equal human beings; that our disabilities are limitations only, and that our identity does not derive from being disabled.

We proclaim that we have the same value as people who are not disabled, and we reject any scheme of labeling or classifying us that encourages people to think of us as having diminished value.

We reject the idea that institutions must be created to "care" for us, and proclaim that these institutions have been used to "manage" us in ways that non-disabled people are not expected to accept. We particularly denounce institutions whose purpose is to punish us for being disabled, or to confine us for the convenience of others.

We reject the notion that we need "experts," to tell us how to live, especially experts from the able-bodied world. We are not diagnoses in need of a cure or cases to be closed. We are human, with human dreams and ambitions. We deny that images of disability are appropriate metaphors for incompetence, stupidity, ugliness or weakness.

We are aware that as people with disabilities, we have been considered objects of charity and we have been considered commodities. We are neither. We reject charitable enterprises that exploit our lifestyle to titillate others, and which propose to establish the rules by which we must live without our participation. We also reject businesses that use us as "warm bodies" to provide a passive market for their services, again laying down rules by which we must live for their profit. We recognize that the lines between charities and businesses are blurred in the disability industry, and we do not accept services from either if their essential function is to exploit us.

We assert our rights of self-determination in the face of rules, eligibility criteria, regulations, customs, laws or other barriers, and we pledge not to allow any authority or institution to deprive us of our freedom of choice.

Finally, we assert that any service we need, from specialized teaching to personal care, can be provided to us in the community among our non-disabled peers. Segregated institutions are not necessary to serve us, and they have been the greatest source of our oppression, especially when they have been run by able-bodied people without our participation.

All human beings are more alike than we are different. We recognize that when we assert this belief we will find ourselves in conflict with regressive institutions and their supporters, some of whom may be disabled themselves. We do not expect thousands of years of stereotyping to dissipate quickly. We commit ourselves and those who come after us to challenge our oppression on every level until we are allowed to be fully human and assert our individuality ahead of our disability.

By John R. Woodward, M.S.W.
Center for Independent Living of North Florida, Inc.

ACKNOWLEDGMENTS

I gratefully acknowledge Minister Willie Henderson for his unwavering faith, fervent prayers, inspiration and encouragement. I also wish to acknowledge, especially, Paula Ryan, Southeastern PASS Cadre and Sally Atwell, Shepherd Spinal Center who had compassion and vision to help me turn my dream into reality when others were going in the opposite direction—thank you.

CONTENTS

PREFACE

The purpose of this book is to inform, educate and inspire Americans with disabilities with inside tips on how to find the easiest, least expensive, and direct-to-the-source alternative resources. While this book is available to all low-income people, it supports people with disabilities who want to improve their quality of life by employment or affordable homeownership.

I also wrote this book to inform other people with disabilities about the ultimate benefit of the Social Security Administration, and other little known government resources to build self-sufficiency and assets—as I did.

Are you living on Social Security Disability Insurance (SSDI) or Supplemental Security Income (SSI) and just getting by? Do you have dreams and aspirations of starting and operating a successful and profitable business or getting a college degree and working in a specific career field? Do you want to live independently in your own home? If you answered yes, you are probably passing up FREE money. You should get every dollar you are entitled to pursue your goals because every little bit helps.

SSA offers a little known program called Plan for Achieving Self Sufficiency (PASS) for SSI and SSDI beneficiaries. If you can show a work goal capable of being accomplished, a well-written PASS application and business plan (for entrepreneurs), it is highly probable you can get a PASS. So, do not pass up this amazing opportunity because PASS offers a way out of poverty.

INTRODUCTION

You have a right to ask for these resources; and it is up to you to apply for a PASS. A PASS can include expenses for a computer, monitor, color printer, fax, copier, supplies, equipment, automobile, gas, maintenance, daycare, books and tuition, tools, adaptive equipment, personal care, cell phone, vehicle modification, special work-related medical expenses, and much more.

Does this all sound too good to be true? It did to me when I heard about PASS. Now that I am informed, I wonder why so many other people with disabilities are not aware of this rehabilitation program, which could possibly motivate them to self-sufficiency.

From my research, there are two primary reasons why PASS is underused. First, PASS is complicated (but do not be discouraged, it is doable). Second, SSA does not do very much to expose it or notify beneficiaries that they are eligible for PASS. However, as you delve into this book, you will uncover the best opportunity available to people with disabilities that are ready to live their dreams.

CHAPTER 1

WHAT IS A PASS?

A PASS is a SSI "Ticket to Work" incentive that a disabled person can use to set aside or save income and or resources for a definite time to achieve an occupational goal and receive an additional SSI check for monthly living expenses.

This time-sensitive program is expected to increase your self-support, measured by higher earnings when your work goal is met.

Helpful Tip: SSA might approve your PASS if you have the potential to earn more than you currently receive in benefits.

For example, if you are receiving SSDI income, PASS helps you keep this income that would otherwise disqualify you from getting SSI. Income can be earned or unearned. SSDI is unearned income that you must set aside in a separate PASS bank account, for the purpose of helping you find and keep a job or start and operate a sustainable business. Spending this money for other purposes may cause your PASS to be permanently suspended. You could have to repay the misappropriated benefits to SSA.

Basically, a PASS application consists of questions that require written and thorough information such as:

- Description of work goal, duties you expect to perform on your job or in your business in light of the limitations you described in your application
- Specific work goal that is reasonable and that you are capable of performing
- A list of steps and milestones in sequence that you will take to reach your work goal
- List of items and services needed to achieve your work goal
- Sources of income and resources to be set aside
- Personal budget that shows monthly living expenses

Helpful Tip: Your living expenses must not exceed monthly SSI benefits prior to applying for PASS. SSA expects you to be living within your SSI income (see example Budget in PASS Kit). With a frugal budget and determination; you can sustain yourself on a meager fixed income with a PASS and not be evicted.

Your PASS application will be reviewed, approved or denied by your local SSA PASS Cadre, and if approved is subject to periodic reviews to monitor possible abuse and compliance.

Your approved PASS includes your agreement to use your monthly (SSDI income) exclusively for your approved PASS expenses. Therefore, SSA will not count that portion of your Social Security as income when they compute your eligibility and payment amount for SSI. Sections 1612 (b) (4) (A-B) and 1613 (a) (4) of the Social Security Act permit the exclusion of income and resources if they are needed to fulfill an approved PASS.

The PASS is a 14-page application form in topic outline format as follows:

- Part I—Your Goal
- Part II—Medical, Vocational, Educational Background
- Part III—Your Plan
- Part IV—Plan Expenditures and Disbursement
- Part V—Income, Resource Exclusion
- Part VI—Remarks
- Part VII—Agreement
- Privacy Act Statement
- Time It Takes To Complete This Form
- Receipt For Your Plan For Achieving Self-Sufficiency
- Your Reporting And Recordkeeping Responsibilities

Other Benefits of Having a PASS

Medicaid is automatic for SSI beneficiaries in most states under an approved PASS. However, you need to check with your PASS specialist to determine your eligibility for Medicaid.

Food Stamps are an added benefit because the federal Food Stamp law does not count income and resources set aside in a PASS. The sticking point may be your ability to explain PASS because some government workers do not understand it; and this may complicate the application process. It is my understanding that the Food and Nutrition Service will exclude PASS income based on Title 7, Chapter 51, Section 2014 (d) (15) of the U.S. Code. However, refer to your local Food Stamp office for specific information about income included in your Food Stamp determination.

Subsidized Housing under Housing and Urban Development (HUD) does not count income and resources set aside in a PASS in determining rent. If you are already in the Section 8 voucher program or living in housing for senior citizens and disabled people, this is a big step in terms of presenting your budget for monthly living expenses. If your expenditures exceed the amount of a monthly SSI payment, you will not qualify for a PASS. The simplest way to explain it is this: The monthly SSI benefit must cover your shelter and food. PASS funds i.e.

SSDI benefits, are deposited in the bank monthly to pay for your PASS expenses. I also understand that HUD will exclude (PASS income) if you get housing assistance. You should contact HUD to find out how your benefits will be affected. Reference: 24 C.F.R. 5.609(c)(8)(i) Revised as of April 1, 2003.

Helpful Tip: Disabled adults who are considering PASS, yet are facing homelessness, can apply for emergency subsidized housing and request priority placement on a waiting list.

Section 811 Supportive Housing for Persons with Disabilities is designed to enable very low-income persons with disabilities to live independently with supportive services. This program is an important part of HUD's overall strategy to protect vulnerable populations from homelessness and sub-standard housing conditions. These housing choices include multi-family rental housing projects, group homes and condominium units for people with disabilities. Such housing is available for very low-income people who are at least 18 years of age with a physical disability, developmental disability, chronic mental illness, or any combination of the three. Residents pay 30 percent of their adjusted monthly income in rent while HUD funds pay the difference between the monthly approved operating cost and the rent received from the tenant.

Helpful Tip: Living with disability can be easier with low-income housing. Minor disabilities may only require ground floor accommodation or an elevator and near supermarket, drug store and public transportation, etc. More extensive impairments may require specific accessibility in handicap housing.

It is interesting to note, the Federal Fair Housing Act and Fair Housing Amendments Act prohibit discrimination against people with physical or mental disabilities and ensure your rights as a disabled tenant in requesting reasonable modification of your dwelling. Under these provisions, a landlord may not reject a prospective tenant with disabilities (including, but not limited to, hearing, mobility and visual impairments, alcoholism being treated through a recovery program, mental illness, HIV, AIDS, and mental retardation).

Landlords are also prohibited from asking questions about your disability or requesting medical records. Evaluation of you may be based on financial stability, history as a tenant, and any criteria that landlord applies to all tenants (such as minimum rent-to-income ratio).☺

Opportunity…often it comes in the form of misfortune, or temporary defeat.

NAPOLEON HILL

CHAPTER 2

WHO CAN GET A PASS?

You can get a PASS if you are a disabled or blind person receiving SSI, under the age of 65 and your PASS is approved. However, disabled people receiving SSDI can use it too. Again, SSDI is considered "unearned income" which you must set aside, in a separate bank account, to pay for work-related expenses if you are approved for a PASS. You will receive SSI to live on.

Before you apply for a PASS, you need to first apply for services at Vocational Rehabilitation (VR) to get whatever financial assistance they can provide before applying for a PASS. Second, you need to get help from your Benefits Navigator Office to determine whether you have exhausted your Trial Work Period (TWP), which were your attempts to test your ability to work. During this period, you will be allowed to keep your paycheck and disability check without having to report it or the amount. A TWP is 9 inconsecutive months. In other words, if you work a couple of months this year, four or five months next year and so forth, the IRS will report your dates of employment and earnings to SSA. You will be required to request a statement of earnings, and after the 9-month TWP, if your gross monthly earnings are below the Substantial Gainful Activity (SGA) level, $850 in 2007, $1500 for a legally blind person, your SSDI will not be affected. If your earnings are above the SGA amount, for example: you earn $900 per month, your SSDI will be continued for a three-month period and then terminated.

Here is how it works when you are under PASS. After the 9th TWP month, SSA will extend your eligibility period for 36 months (3 years). You will receive your benefits for each month your gross earnings are less than the SGA amount. During this period, you will be entitled to continued benefits for a 3-month grace period. For the remaining 36 months, you will receive benefits when earnings are below the SGA amount; and you will lose benefits each month your earnings are above the SGA amount.

Complete a PASS application that shows how you will use 100% of your SSDI check for PASS expenses, and then you have, technically, "no income". Therefore, you are entitled to receive SSI benefits to live on. Anyone who receives SSI, SSDI and less than 65 years old can apply for PASS.

Helpful Tip: Be prepared to provide answers to these questions to your PASS specialist. What will you be doing while saving for your PASS? If your goal is business startup, will you be running it out of your home? What is your contingency plan in case you cannot continue with your PASS? Will you attend seminars related to your career field or business enterprise? ☺

The world is full of willing people, some willing to work, the rest willing to let them.

ROBERT FROST

CHAPTER 3

PASS EXPENSES

A PASS must show how your savings will be spent to achieve your work goal.

Part III or your plan lists the steps, in sequence that you will take to reach your work goal. Be as specific as possible. For example, if you will be attending school, show the courses you will study each quarter and semester. Include the final steps to find a job once you have obtained the tools, education, services, etc., that you need.

Part IV of your PASS lists expenses that must be reasonable cost estimates for items and or services and show how the cost was calculated. Examples of my expenses were business license, liability insurance, office supplies and equipment, computer, fax, printer, copier, cell phone, professional services, uniforms, embroidery, company vehicle, and much more.

A PASS could become your "Ticket to Work", with increased monthly income to pay for expenses and shelter. It could also become a passport to reach your vocational destination. If you have been thinking about fulfilling your occupational goal, check out these sample goals accomplished by other people with disabilities:

- Complete bachelor's degree to become a consultant
- Computer specialist

- Apply to law school to become a lawyer
- Marriage, family, child counselor
- Budget analyst
- Start a lawn care business
- Obtain diploma and job in medical administration
- Complete degree at the college of your choice and seek employment
- Complete degree and become a graphics programmer
- Attend a university to become a theater administrator
- Work part-time as a housekeeper, custodian, janitor, maintenance worker
- Multimedia, video production developer
- Attend school to learn car repair
- Maintain, keep your job
- Licensed real estate agent
- Arts, crafts decorative artist
- Attend school to become an accounting assistant
- Environmental scientist
- Certified drafter
- Accounting clerk
- Train field dogs for hunting
- Paralegal
- Part-time employment as shipping, receiving clerk
- Clerical work at Wal-Mart
- Biotechnology lab technician
- Newspaper or magazine journalist
- Video production degree to become a technician
- Housecleaning service

Social Security Resources are Rightfully Yours

SSA allows you to claim thousands of dollars in benefits that you can use to develop your own employment plan. If you can earn part or all of your living, it is in the best interests of our government to support you, even if you have to continue to receive part, or all of your benefits, to subsidize your employment. People who use PASS (such as I) go from being benefits-recipients to wage-earners and taxpayers, returning back to the government some or all of what we received.

In choosing the expenditures to be included in your PASS and filing the documents to support it, it is important for you to remember that "grey areas" and "questionable items" can mean trouble. If you are not sure that an item is something you include under your PASS, check with your PASS specialist at SSA PASS Cadre or leave it out. Do not jeopardize a good PASS by trying to push it over the limit.

Examples of Possible PASS Expenditures:

- Start-up capital and inventory required to establish a business
- Any cost associated with an educational or occupational training program
- Attendant care and personal assistance
- Child care
- Equipment or tools, specific to the individual's condition or general use
- Uniforms including dress business clothing, safety equipment
- Least costly alternatives for transportation including public transportation
- Hire of private or commercial carriers
- Purchase of a private vehicle
- Dues and publications for academic or professional purposes
- Modifications to buildings or vehicles to accommodate a person's disability
- Licenses, certifications, permits necessary for employment or self-employment☺

Money for me has only one sound: liberty.

GABRIELLE CHANEL

CHAPTER 4

WHO CAN WRITE A PASS?

A PASS is very flexible. SSA suggests that you obtain outside help to prepare a PASS application, since you are required to prove you are capable of performing the work you plan to do; and that your plan to start work is reasonable. I wrote my own PASS. You may wish to consult your local VR office or Goodwill, but this is not required.

Helpful Tip: SSA personnel are required to write your PASS if you ask them to do it. But, they may not be as knowledgeable about your disability or capabilities.

A PASS can make you a self-advocate. Therefore, you can write your own PASS. From my experience, this is a blessing and a curse. You must be committed to write a thorough and concise application that you will need to update as needed. A PASS is somewhat of a grant proposal. In terms of compliance, it is critical to keep ALL receipts to account for every penny you spend to obtain your occupational goal. Whoever writes your PASS must:

- Write a detail plan specifying your work goal that you can reasonably attain;
- Determine the time limit to reach your goal;
- State how PASS income and resources set aside will be spent and accounted for; and
- Describe any goods and services needed to reach your goal; and why these items are needed.

SSA Just Might Approve Your PASS for a Business

If you have aspirations of starting a business, you must write a detail and feasible (doable) business plan as well. When feasibility is questionable, SSA may require corroboration from an authoritative source. Since I wrote my own business plan, I submitted it to The University of Georgia Small Business Development Center for evaluation and feasibility support.

Helpful Tip: You must do "due diligence" in researching the market segment and financials.

Need Help Writing Your Business Plan?

If you need help writing a business plan, get books on the subject at the library or pay someone to write it for you. This expense can be written into your PASS. The business plan is a step-by-step plan of action you need to understand from beginning to end. It will require a lot of writing, re-writing and input for you or someone else to put it in the right format.

Fees charged by PASS preparers range from $200 to $800. Some preparers charge additional fees for preparing amendments and monitoring; and these are acceptable PASS expenses as well.☺

Money can't buy you happiness, but it does bring you a more pleasant form of misery.

SPIKE MILLIGAN

CHAPTER 5

BEFORE YOU GET STARTED

Start planning how you will use a PASS long before you are ready to apply for it or look for a job. Your first step should be to research the different work incentives in great detail. Your second step should be to contact your local VR office and sign up for services and assistance with business start-up or vocational training funds.

Another key point before getting started is this: If you are not willing to keep records, you should not bother to apply for PASS. You need to keep receipts or cancelled checks until SSA contacts you to find out if you are still following your PASS. When they contact you, they will ask to see the receipts or cancelled checks. If you are **not** following your PASS, you may have to pay back some or all of the SSI you received.

Start planning a records management system to keep records on all your income and expenditures under PASS. These records enable you to prove that you are spending your benefits properly when your case is reviewed. It will also make completing forms more efficient.

Helpful Tip: When a PASS is denied based on feasibility concerns, SSA's PASS Cadre specialist must inform you whether it is the goal or the plan that is not considered feasible. Before denying a plan as not feasible, the PASS specialist must contact you to explain why your PASS is not capable of being done, and discuss changes that would make the plan doable.☺

There is no scarcity of opportunity to make a living at what you love; there's only scarcity of resolve to make it happen.

WAYNE DYER

CHAPTER 6

APPLYING AND FOLLOWING A PASS

A PASS is a formal application procedure. Call or go online to request a PASS form from your local SSA office. At the end of this book, you will find a sample PASS and forms for you to study.

The PASS specialist reviewing your application will decide whether to deny or approve it. They are responsible for assuring there is a good chance you can meet your occupational goal; and that the resources and services you want are needed and cost effective.

PASS Reporting and Recordkeeping

If your PASS is approved, you must tell SSA about any changes to your plan. You must tell them if:

- Your medical condition improves or declines;
- Your occupational goal changes;

- You need to change your budget or select vendors;
- You are unable to follow your PASS;
- You decide not to pursue your goal or decide to pursue a different goal;
- You decide that you do not need to pay for any of the expenses you listed in your PASS;
- Someone else pays for any of your PASS expenses;
- Your employment status changed;
- Your representative payee or your address changes;
- You use the income or resources SSA excludes for a purpose other than the expense specified in the PASS;
- You decide you need to pay for other expenses not listed in your PASS.

If you do not tell your PASS specialist about these changes within 10 days following the month it happened, they might suspend (stop) your plan.

SSA also recommends that you pay all your expenses by check, from your PASS account, to develop a proper paper trail. Always record the check number each time you enter a PASS expense into your log.

A sample Income Log appears at the end of this book. You can use it to record all your income, from whatever source.

Records You Need to Keep:
- Written PASS application with all amendments;
- All receipts, invoices, paychecks, bank statements and other financial records that are an income and expense record;
- Month-by-month narrative of progress toward completing your PASS; and
- Complete record of your correspondence with SSA (a couple of paragraphs listing your PASS activities for the month will do it. It could be as simple as a list of places you applied for work or a statement that you attended all your classes during the month.

There are Penalties for Noncompliance
SSA will review your PASS frequently to determine if you are still eligible for the benefits you receive, usually quarterly. The frequency of your reviews will be determined by the nature of your disability. This is an 18-month program with an option to extend it for 6-months to reach your goal. If the PASS proposal is denied, you have a right to appeal.

DISABILITY EMPOWERMENT

If your PASS lapses into noncompliance because you are not balancing your PASS bank account, SSA will suspend your PASS and give you an opportunity to request an amendment. Or, as a last option, they might terminate your PASS. If you are found noncompliant, you might have to repay the additional benefits you received during your PASS.

How to Request a PASS Plan Amendment

If your work goal or PASS changes, you can request to amend your PASS by editing your original PASS by typing "PASS Amendment" at the top of the application; then type all changed information on the form and highlight all the changes. Enclose a cover letter with the amendment explaining why the amendments are necessary. Or, follow the specific instructions of your PASS Cadre specialist.

How to Request a PASS Extension

If you need more time to complete your PASS or edit your original PASS, type "PASS Extension" on the top of the application, then type all changes and highlight the changed information. Include a cover letter explaining why more time is needed.

Working Will Affect Your Benefits

Aforementioned, under SSDI rules, you can have a "Trial Work Period". This means you can test yourself to see if you can work without having to worry right away that you will lose your disability benefits. The trial work period can be no longer than 9 months, during which you spend more than 40 hours on the job if you are employed. Once you have completed 9 trial work months in any 60-month period, SSA will review your earnings to determine if you remain eligible for SSDI. The significant factor will be whether your average earnings during the trial period were greater than $850 per month.

If your average earnings have been at least $850 per month on a regular basis, SSA will continue your benefits for three more months and then will cut off all benefits. SSA can reinstate your benefits in full anytime within the next 36 months, if your earnings go down below the $850 level. This period is called the extended period of eligibility because during these 36 months, you can receive your full SSDI check for any month that your earnings fall below $850, or if you lose your job.

Addresses of SSA's Regional PASS Cadres

PASS proposals are reviewed by a "cadre" of PASS specialists. They are specially trained SSA personnel whose primary job is to review PASS proposals.

REGION 1
Regional Commissioner, SSA
Attn: Disability Programs
Room 1100
JFK Federal Building
Cambridge Street
Boston, MA 02203

REGION 2
Regional Commissioner, SSA
Attn: Disability Programs
Room 40-102
Federal Building
26 Federal Plaza
New York, NY 10278

REGION 3
Regional Commissioner, SSA
Attn: Disability Programs
P.O. Box 8788
Philadelphia, PA 19104

REGION 4
Regional Commissioner, SSA
Attn: Disability Programs
P.O. Box 902
Atlanta, GA 30323

REGION 5
Regional Commissioner, SSA
Attn: Disability Programs
10th Floor
105 Adams Street
Chicago, IL 60603

REGION 6
Regional Commissioner, SSA
Attn: Disability Programs
Room 1440
1200 Main Tower Building
Dallas, TX 75202

REGION 7
Regional Commissioner, SSA
Attn: Disability Programs
Room 436, FOB
Kansas City, MO 64106

REGION 8
Regional Commissioner, SSA
Attn: Disability Programs
Room 1194, FOB
Denver, CO 80294

REGION 9
Regional Commissioner, SSA
Attn: Disability Programs
75 Hawthorne Street
San Francisco, CA 94105

REGION 10
Regional Commissioner
SSA
Attn: Disability Programs
2001 Sixth Avenue, M-S RX-50
Seattle, WA 98121

One's best success comes after his greatest disappointments.

HENRY WARD BEECHER

CHAPTER 7

ALTERNATIVE RESOURCE DIRECTORY

Creative Strategies

Finding Alternative Resources

As a disabled person, starting a business, purchasing a home or meeting your responsibilities may require you to ask your community e.g. United Way for assistance and referrals. Your community offers a wide range of services to assist disabled individuals and families with personal trial, but do not assume they know what you need.

Financial Support

General Assistance (GA) is a program financed entirely through local state funds to provide for the support of individuals who have a low income, or disabled people who have demonstrated a need. For example, a Social Security disability applicant with psychiatric disabilities and do not get Social Security benefits, even though you have little or no income can apply for these financial benefits because you may be waiting for your application to be approved or SSA does not consider you to be disabled. As an applicant, you should apply for GA (also known as General Relief), since these funds do not require a finding of disability. You must apply at your county welfare office. Applications are generally processed within 45 days. General Assistance benefits vary from state to state, county to county but are consistently low, averaging from $200 to $250 per month for a single person. State law permits counties to limit General Assistance to three months per year. Some states may not offer General Assistance.

State Supplements are optional supplements provided by most states to help persons meet needs not fully covered by federal SSI payments. For example, California, a very generous state, pays a monthly supplement of $362 for an individual on top of the federal contribution. Each state determines whether it will make a payment, to whom, and in what amount. These supplements, paid on a regular monthly basis, are intended to cover such items as food, shelter, clothing, utilities, and other daily necessities determined by the individual states. Some states provide optional supplementary payments to all persons eligible for SSI benefits. Others may limit them to certain SSI recipients such as the blind or residents of domiciliary care facilities, or they may extend payments to persons ineligible for SSI because of excess income. For additional information, contact your local SSA office.

Qualified Medicare Beneficiaries Assistance (QMB) is a Q Track class of assistance (COA) that provides a Medicare supplement to individuals who meet financial criteria based on the Federal Poverty Level. QMB pays the following for the QMB eligible individual:

- The monthly premium for Part A Medicare for those individuals who must pay a premium
- The monthly premium for Part B Medicare
- All Medicare co-insurance payments (the 20% of covered charges that Medicare will not pay)
- All Medicare deductibles, such as the in-patient hospital deductible.

QMB will not cover any medical service that is not covered by Medicare. Applicants for QMB must meet all eligibility criteria for this COA in the month of approval and the following month in order to be approved. No property search is required for this class of assistance.

The standard of promptness for QMB applications is 10 working days from receipt of the application. A face-to-face contact and office interview is not required at initial application or annual re-determination. For all applications and annual re-determinations: Your statement of income and resources provided on the application and review form is acceptable verification. No further verification is required unless questionable. Call your local welfare office to apply.

Individual Development Account (IDA) is a saving's account in which you receive a savings match of up to five times the original deposit. In most cases, IDAs are used for starting a business, first home purchase or post-secondary education. Each IDA program may have different requirements to participate. Most common guidelines include employment earnings, net worth, earned-income level and participation in financial education training. A general rule of thumb is that you be at least within the household income guideline of 200 percent of poverty (as defined by the federal government). Programs may also require qualification for Temporary Assistance for Needy Families (TANF) or the Earned Income Tax Credit. Check with your local United Way or other participating organization for details.

IDA Integration with Other Programs

Plan for Achieving Self Sufficiency can be used to increase flexibility for a person receiving SSI and SSDI and wants to participate in an IDA program. If you have a PASS and are participating in an IDA program, funds from the IDA can only be used for the specified work goal outlined in a PASS. SSA excludes money placed in a PASS as counting as assets and income.

Supplemental Security Income is designed to help people with disabilities that have little or no income. SSI beneficiaries can participate in any asset-building program as long as they meet the program qualifications and are mindful of asset limits that can jeopardize benefits. You cannot have more than $2,000 in assets as an individual or $3,000 if married. (Assets include any readily available cash such as a savings account.) Your benefits may be reduced or you may not be eligible at all if you have other sources of income. Income SSA includes are such things as:

- Money that you earn from employment
- Pensions, alimony, and interest
- Food, clothing, or shelter that is given to you on a regular basis
- An amount of money that SSA assumes is given to you by someone else or if they live with you and have their own income—similar to TANF rules.

Social Security Disability Insurance pays benefits to disabled individuals who have paid sufficiently into Social Security. There are no restrictions for SSDI recipients who want to accumulate assets. Also, there are no limits under the SSDI program on the amount of unearned income you may receive. However, earnings levels will affect your benefits. The "earnings threshold" is fixed nationally, not by state.

Earned Income Tax Credit (EITC) is a federal income tax credit for low income working individuals and families. The credit may reduce the amount of federal tax owed. The EITC can help IDA participants reach their savings goals that allow a tax credit to be matched when deposited into the IDA account. Income and family size determine the amount of the EITC. The rate differs depending on the number of children in the family. The EITC does not generally affect eligibility for any public benefits.

Down Payment Assistance Grants

People with disabilities can become successful homeowners. If you are using an IDA to save for down payment assistance to purchase a home, you can combine funding from a number of sources. Grants generally do not need to be repaid and may come from sources such as city affordable housing programs.

American Dream Downpayment Initiative (ADDI) will provide down payment, closing costs, and home rehabilitation assistance to eligible individuals. ADDI

DISABILITY EMPOWERMENT

provides qualifying borrowers with $10,000 to serve as a down payment at zero percent interest. It is basically a deferred second mortgage loan that will be forgiven if you continue to live in and own your home for at least 5 years, without refinancing it. The second mortgage loan must be repaid in full if at any time the borrower sells the property, refinances or no longer occupies the property within 5 years of purchasing the property. This program can be combined with other down-payment assistance programs that might be available. The home rehabilitation must be completed within one year of the home purchase. Home rehabilitation may include, but is not limited to, the reduction of lead paint hazards and the remediation of other home health hazards. Contact your city and county housing office.

NeighborWorks is a national network of more than 225 community-based organizations that offer a variety of programs to assist disabled individuals purchase and maintain their homes. Many NeighborWorks organizations offer downpayment assistance as well as home repair programs. To locate a NeighborWorks organization in your area, visit their website and click on "NeighborWorks Lookup."

Affordable Mortgage Loans

Neighborhood Assistance Corporation of America (NACA) is a national non-profit community advocacy and housing services organization. As a result of its advocacy, NACA can offer you the Best Mortgage in America with over $10 Billion committed to its home ownership program. They plan to eventually offer auto loans and credit cards. Lowest interest rate. No down payment. No closing costs. No fees. No perfect credit. The NACA mortgage is a revolutionary product that can be used for:

- Purchase: Buying an existing home, new construction, single or multi-family home, condo or co-op;
- Purchase and Rehab: Purchasing a home needing repairs and financing the cost of the renovation;

- Refinancing: Available to homeowners saddled with a predatory loan.

For more information, go to www.naca.com or call Toll Free: 1-888-302-6222 (naca)

Rural Housing Service Loans (RHS) formerly known as the Farmers Home Administration, a branch of the U.S. Department of Agriculture (USDA), offers mortgage loans with no down payment requirement and with low interest rates to low-income and disabled families and market interest rates to moderate-income families who live in rural areas.

- Section 502 Direct Loan Program—is available to lower income individuals and families who wish to live in rural areas or rural cities or towns. Under the program, individuals or families receive a loan directly from Rural Development. Payments are based on income, with no downpayment required. You must be unable to obtain a homeownership loan from a bank or other conventional sources.
- No Downpayment—is required for a USDA direct housing loan. The standard term for a loan is 33 years for most borrowers. However, 38-year loans are available to those who cannot afford a 33-year loan. The interest rate for direct housing loans is set by Rural Development office; and they can estimate the interest rate you would pay.
- The Mutual Self-Help Housing Program—families provide a substantial portion of the labor involved in building their own homes. This "sweat equity" contribution reduces the total cost of purchasing a home—allowing many disabled people to purchase houses that otherwise would have been out of reach. Also, because it brings different families together to work on each other's houses, the program builds and strengthens the ties of community. It is active

throughout the country and helps some 1,500 rural families build their own homes each year.

- Home Improvement and Repair Assistance—if you are already a rural homeowner and your house needs repairs, or modifications to make it accessible to a person with a disability, you may be eligible for home improvement or repair assistance through USDA Rural Development.
- Single-Family Housing Home Improvement Loans (Section 502)—in addition to providing loan funds for the purchase of a house, the Section 502 Single Family Housing Direct Loan program can help lower income rural homeowners make vital improvements to their homes. Section 502 loans are available to make substantial home repairs when other loan options are not available.
- Home Repair Loan and Grant Programs (Section 504)—is for families and individuals with very low incomes. Rural Development makes loans for repairs, to improve or modernize a home, make it safer or more sanitary, or to remove health hazards. For seniors 62 and older who cannot afford a loan, grant funds are available for these repairs. The most common types of repairs financed by the Section 504 program include fixing or replacing roofs, modernizing heating and wiring systems, and making houses accessible to people with disabilities. You can also apply for funds to install insulation and storm windows, put in a septic system, and install or repair a bathroom. The maximum amount you can borrow under the Section 504 Home Repair Loan program is $20,000. The interest rate for these loans is 1 percent and is limited to very-low-income, rural residents whose incomes fall below 50 per cent of the area's median income.
- Housing Preservation Grant Program—allows nonprofit organizations, public bodies, and Native American tribes to renovate deteriorating homes and rental properties using grants from Rural

Development. Grant funds are used to repair and bring up to code properties occupied by families with low incomes.

Check with your local RHS office or a local lender for eligibility requirements, or contact Fannie Mae HomePath^{SM} Services at 1-800-7FANNIE (or 1-800-732-6643).

Plan for Achieving Self Sufficiency—allows you to write mortgage payment into a PASS for a person with a home-based business.

Deferred Payment and Forgivable Loans

HomeChoice—is the first national mortgage product tailored exclusively to the needs of borrowers with disabilities. This is a 50-million dollar underwriting for single-family houses designed to accommodate the mortgage underwriting needs of individuals with disabilities and families who have a member with a disability. HomeChoice's underwriting criteria use flexibility never before seen in the lending industry. Contact your state housing development office for details.

Affordable New Homes

Habitat for Humanity International builds affordable housing for low-income and disabled families. Houses are sold at no profit, with no interest charged on the mortgage. Homeowners are responsible for making a down payment and monthly mortgage payments. In exchange for your Habitat house, homeowners must invest several hundred hours of your own labor and sweat equity into building your Habitat house and the houses of others. Contrary to popular belief, there is no waiting list—in Atlanta, GA. To learn more about your local program, contact your local Habitat Affiliate.

Tax Benefits

Low-income people under age 65 who are retired on permanent and total disability may be able to claim a federal tax credit.

Credit for the Elderly or the Disabled

- You can take the credit for the elderly or the disabled if:
- You are a qualified individual, and
- Your income is not more than certain limits.

You are a qualified individual for this credit if you are a U.S. citizen or resident alien and, at the end of the tax year, you are:

1. Age 65 or older, or
2. Under age 65, retired on permanent and total disability, and
   a. Received taxable disability income, and
   b. Did not reach mandatory retirement age before the tax year.

You are retired on permanent and total disability if:

- You were permanently and totally disabled when you retired, and
- You retired on disability before the close of the tax year.

Even if you do not retire formally, you may be considered retired on disability when you have stopped working because of your disability.

Permanently and totally disabled means you are permanently and totally disabled if you cannot engage in any substantial gainful activity because of your physical or mental condition. A physician must certify that the condition has lasted or can be expected to last continuously for 12 months or more, or that the condition can be expected to result in death. Substantial gainful activity is the performance of significant duties over a reasonable period of time while working for pay or profit, or in work generally done for pay or profit.

Property Tax Exemption (Basic Homestead) once granted is automatically renewed each year as long as you continually occupy the home under the same ownership. The home must be your legal residence for all purposes including the registration of your vehicles and the filing of your income tax. You cannot file for homestead exemption on rental property, vacant land or on more than one property.

In addition to basic homestead exemption there are additional exemptions for residents age 62 and older and/or disabled and disabled veterans. You must apply for these exemptions in person. To be eligible, you must be permanently and totally disabled and receiving Social Security disability benefits for a property exemption if the county in which you live adopts an ordinance to this effect. You must provide the tax assessor's office with proof of total disability.

Deductions from Income determine your taxable income. People with disabilities can deduct medical expenses that exceed 7.5% of their adjusted gross income. Medical expenses include payments made to diagnose, cure, treat or prevent a disease or treat any body or bodily function. Deductions also include transportation to medical care, health insurance payments, and the following costs:

- Artificial limbs, eyeglasses, and hearing aids, special telephone equipment for people with hearing impairments, closed captioning equipment for TVs
- Wheelchair purchase and maintenance
- Guide animal acquisition and care
- Home improvements whose main purpose is medical care (e.g. wheelchair ramp) as long as it does not increase the home's value
- An employee with a physical or mental disability that functionally limits his employment may be able to deduct impairment-related work expenses.

Capital Gains Taxes When Selling a Home

A homeowner is allowed to sell a principal residence once every two years and exclude up to $250,000 ($500,000 for a married couple) of the gain on the sale. If you meet the two-year ownership and use tests for a principal residence and do not sell more than one principal residence in a two-year period, you can exclude any capital gains tax on the sale.

Federal Debt and Student Loan Cancellation

A federal government debt can be "forgiven" (or written off) by the federal government under certain circumstances. These circumstances include the borrower's school closes while you are attending, the borrower becomes permanently disabled, or the borrower becomes deceased. Documentation of the situation is required and eligibility is determined by the guarantor.

Jobs for Disabled People

The following list of associations and organizations offer numerous services to people with physical or mental disabilities. Many offer job placement services, provide on-site accessibility surveys, job analysis and offer advice and support to people with disabilities. Contact individual listings for details of services provided:

- **American Cancer Society**—Refers employers to organizations offering help in recruiting qualified individuals with disabilities, and community programs offering consultation and technical assistance to cancer patients, survivors, and their families. Publishes information on the employment of cancer patients and survivors. 1-800-ACS-2345, http://www.cancer
- **American Council of the Blind**—Provides information on job openings and topics affecting the employment of individuals who are blind and visually impaired, including job seeking strategies, job accommodations, electronic aids, and employment discrimination. Offers free legal assistance in employment discrimination cases. American Council of the Blind, 1155 15th Street, NW, Suite 720, Washington, D.C. 20005, 202-467-5081 or 1-800-424-8666, http://www.acb.org
- **disABLEDperson, Inc**—If you have a disability, this website will assist you in many areas. This web portal is all inclusive with links to topics including job boards, learning disability, social security disability, the American with Disability Act, developmental disability, physical disability, emotional disability, mental disability, disabled veterans, disabled women and more. Food and Diet are also an important part of this web portal with updated information on nutrition, metabolism, diet and weight loss. http://www.disABLEDperson.com
- **Project ABLE**—operates through the joint efforts of several federal agencies. It provides a national resume bank of qualified individuals on the

DISABILITY EMPOWERMENT

disability rolls who want to work. It has provided an easily accessible applicant pool to employers through Office of Personnel Management. Do you receive SSI and/or SSDI and are ABLE to work or to return to work? Project ABLE can provide information on how you may be ABLE to temporarily keep your benefits while you try to work. Project ABLE is a federally-funded initiative administered in partnership with state and private organizations. This project is designed to educate and assist individuals with disabilities receiving SSI/SSDI regarding the impact of employment on various State and Federal benefits they receive.

IBM Project ABLE—Is an IBM Diversity recruitment program offering people with disabilities the chance to explore IBM careers nationwide. They can provide the opportunities that will enable you to reach your career goals!

Typical openings within IBM are:

Electrical Engineering	Mechanical Engineering
Computer Science	Management Information System
Computer Engineering	Technical Marketing and Sales
Computer Information Systems	Finance
Industrial Engineering	Business Administration

You can apply either directly to IBM or through one of the organizations listed below. IBM sources qualified candidates with disabilities through these organizations. The Americans with Disabilities Act (ADA) does not allow employers to ask candidates to self-identify. These organizations are one way IBM outreach to qualified candidates with disabilities.

http://www.benderconsult.com/opp/
http://ehrweb.aaas.org/entrypoint/
http://www.lift-inc.org/
http://www.business-disability.com/index.aspx

- **U.S. State Department Student Disability Program**—A job. A chance. A future. If you are a student with a disability, the Department of State may want to employ you. In an effort to increase the hires of people with disabilities the Department has partnered with the Department of Labor, Office of Disability Employment and Policy, and the U.S. Department of Defense, who administer the Workforce Recruitment Program for College Students with Disabilities (WRP). The purpose of the program is to attract and refer talented students with disabilities to federal and private sector organizations for temporary and permanent employment.

Students are interviewed on campuses across the country and names are placed in a database available to participating federal agencies. Grade level is determined by the number of college credits and experience obtained at the time of employment, and hiring is done under the Student Temporary appointment for the summer only.

Eligibility Requirements
To be eligible for participation, you must be a U.S. citizen, have a substantial disability, and be enrolled or accepted for enrollment as a degree seeking student at an accredited institution of higher learning on a substantially full-time basis (unless the severity of the disability precludes you from taking a substantially full-time load) or have graduated with a degree from such an institution within the past year. Contact U.S. Department of State, HR/REE/REC, 2401 E Street NW, Suite 518 H, Washington, D.C. 20522, via E-mail:

1. Careers@state.gov: General recruitment and medical clearance questions
2. FSMentors@state.gov: Contact a Foreign Service Officer or Foreign Service Specialist Mentor to learn more about life in the Foreign Service

3. Securityclearance@state.gov: Security clearance and e-QIP questions

For technical issues with the Gateway to State Online Application System, please contact the help desk via E-mail (mgshelp@monster.com) or phone (866-656-6830) if you are having technical difficulties.

Magazines and Reports with Federal Job Ads

- **Ability Magazine**—ABILITY Magazine provides information on new technologies, the "Americans with Disability Act", travel and leisure, employment opportunities for people with disabilities, human interest stories, national and local resource centers and more. ABILITY Magazine helps remove the misunderstandings and erase the stereotypes that surround disability issues. Call or visit their web site for subscription rates. Ability also offers an electronic classified system, **JobAccess**, which allows employers to recruit qualified individuals with disabilities. The goal of **JobAccess** is to enable people with disabilities to enhance their professional lives by providing a dedicated system for finding employment. People with disabilities can locate viable employment opportunities through their print magazine or visit their excellent internet web site at http://www.jobaccess.org, Jobs Information Service, 1001 West 17th St., Costa Mesa, CA 92627, 949-854-8700

- **People with Disabilities in the Federal Government, an Employment Guide**—Published by OPM October 1999. This comprehensive 53 page guide can be downloaded from OPM. The guide is intended to help Federal employers and human resource personnel understand issues and programs aimed at improving the employment of people with disabilities.

Alternate Employment and Vocational Rehabilitation Networks

SSA has implemented the use of alternate VR providers that can supply needed employment and rehabilitation services when the state VR offices do not accept the referral. To date, over 400 providers have signed contracts to provide these services. You can request information on employment networks and state Vocational Rehabilitation Agencies which have agreed to serve your area. Contact MAXIMUS Ticket to Work, P.O. Box 25105, Alexandria, VA 22313-5105, 1-866-968-7842, http://www.yourtickettowork.com

Check with your local and state government for other affordable housing programs and resources for people with disabilities.☺

A bank is a place where they lend you an umbrella in fair weather and ask for it back when it begins to rain.

ROBERT FROST

CHAPTER 8

SUMMARY

A PASS is an income and resource exclusion program that allows you, a person who is disabled or blind, under age 65, to set aside income and or resources for an occupational objective.

A PASS can help you establish or maintain SSI eligibility and also can increase or help maintain your SSI check amount as you gain the capacity for self-support.

SSI will not count the income or resources that are set aside in a PASS when they figure your SSI payment amount.

Requirements for Applying for a PASS:
- Must be approved by SSA PASS Cadre in your State's Region
- Will be reviewed periodically to assure plan is working
- Money set aside in a PASS will not be considered a resource by SSI, Medicaid, HUD, Food Stamps, etc.
- Recommend utilizing SSA 545 Form

DISABILITY EMPOWERMENT

There are tens of thousands of people who could benefit from a PASS. If you really want to work, you do not have to rely solely on assistance from VR. From my experience some VR employees are not as knowledgeable about a PASS. Also, SSA employees are subject to career penalties for approving an erroneous PASS, so everyone tends to be cautious. They do not want to approve a PASS before you are ready, or discontinue benefits you are still entitled. What good is getting a PASS if you end up losing it? If you do as I suggest; I believe you will have success.

If for some unfortunate reason you cannot reach your work goal at the end of a PASS, you will not be penalized if:

- You followed your PASS steps to reach your goal as established and or revised;
- Spent the set aside funds (savings) as outlined in a PASS;
- Kept records of the expenses including receipts; and
- Actively sought employment at the end of a PASS.

SSA needs to spread the word about a PASS because it is really an amazing program. Also, disabled people like me and the professionals, who help us, need to become advocates to:

1. Educate ourselves and each other about a PASS program and;
2. Insist on the benefits that we are entitled to, even if they are denied to us time after time.

If you are interested in pursuing a PASS but have high medical costs, this program could mean a new horizon. Without Medicare and Medicaid, disabled people could choose not to work because they do not want to lose health coverage. You now have the basic ingredients of success that I have outlined in this book for the PASS to be approved.☺

Prosperity is not without many fears and distastes, and adversity is not without comforts and hopes.

FRANCIS BACON

CHAPTER 9

GLOSSARY

Affordable Housing—Where the occupant pays no more than 30% of gross income for total housing costs, including utilities.

Benefit Planning and Assistance (Benefits Navigator Office)—The law directs Social Security to establish a community based work incentives planning and assistance program to disseminate accurate information about work incentives.

Blind Work Expenses for SSI—Earned income that a blind individual uses to meet the expenses of working does not count when we determine SSI eligibility and payment amount. The expenses do not need to be related to blindness and include earned income used to pay income taxes, meals consumed during work hours, transportation costs or guide dog expenses.

Continuation of Medicaid Eligibility for SSI—Medicaid may continue for SSI recipients who are blind or disabled and earn over the SSI limits if they cannot afford similar medical care and depend on Medicaid in order to work.

Continuation of SSI—Working SSI recipients who are blind or disabled may continue to receive payments until countable income exceeds SSI limits.

Continuation of Medicare for SSDI—If Social Security disability payments stop because a person has earnings at or above the substantial gainful activity level, but the person is still disabled, Medicare can continue for at least 93 months after the trial work period. After that, the person can buy Medicare coverage by paying a monthly premium.

Disability Reviews Postponed—Effective January 1, 2001, an individual using a "ticket" will not need to undergo the regularly scheduled disability reviews. A review may be triggered by earnings, however. The following year, January 1, 2002, Social Security disability beneficiaries who have been receiving benefits for at least 24 months will not be asked to go through a disability review because of the work they are doing. However, regularly scheduled medical reviews could still be performed and benefits could be terminated if earnings were above the limits.

Demonstration Projects and Studies—Social Security will conduct a demonstration project to test reducing Social Security disability insurance benefits by $1 for each $2 that a beneficiary earns over a certain amount.

Expansion of Medicaid—States now have the option to expand Medicaid coverage to working individuals with disabilities using income and resource limits set by the states.

Expansion of Medicare—The law expands Medicare hospital insurance coverage to at least 93 months after the trial work period for most disability beneficiaries who work.

Expedited Benefits—As of January 1, 2001, if a beneficiary's benefits have ended because of earning from work and he or she becomes unable to work again because of his or her medical condition within 60 months, benefits may begin again without a new application.

Employment Support Representative—The law calls for the Social security Administration to establish a corps of work incentives specialists in field offices.

Extended Period of Eligibility (SSDI)—For at least three years after a successful trial work period, a Social Security beneficiary who is blind or disabled may receive a disability benefit for any month that his/her earnings are below the substantial gainful activity level (in 2007, $830 for people who are disabled, $1,500 for people who are blind).

Impairment-Related Work Expenses (SSDI)—Certain expenses for things a person with a disability needs because of his or her impairment in order to work may be deducted when counting earnings to determine if the person is performing substantial gainful activity.

Impairment-Related Work Expenses (SSI)—Certain expenses for things a person with a disability needs because of his or her impairment in order to work may be deducted when counting earnings to determine if a person is eligible and to figure the payment amount. For working persons who are blind, the work expenses need not be related to the impairment.

Fair Market Rent—An amount determined by HUD to be the cost of modest, non-luxury rental units in a specific market area. Generally, an "affordable" rent is considered to be below the Fair Market Rent. For example, if the Fair Market Rent is 984.00 per month, you will pay only 30% of your gross monthly income: $523 (income) per month minus 30% is $156.90.

Plan for Achieving Self-Support (SSI)—An SSI recipient who is blind or disabled may set aside income and resources toward an approved plan for achieving self-support.

Protection and Advocacy—The law authorizes Social Security to make payments to protection and advocacy systems in each state to provide legal advice and services to disability beneficiaries.

Recovery During Vocational Rehabilitation (SSDI)—If a person recovers while participating in a vocational rehabilitation program that is likely to lead to becoming self-supporting, benefits may continue until the program ends.

Recovery During Vocational Rehabilitation (SSI)—If a person recovers while participating in a vocational rehabilitation program that is likely to lead to becoming self-supporting, benefits may continue until the program ends.

Special Rules for Persons Who are Blind (SSDI)—Several special rules apply to working beneficiaries who are blind. For example, in 2007, they can earn up to $1,500 before their benefits are affected.

Students with Disabilities (SSI)—Tuition, books and other expenses related to getting an education may not be counted as income for recipients who go to school or are in a training program. Student may exclude up to $1,410 of earnings a month ($5,670 a year).

Subsidies and Special Conditions (SSDI)—Refer to support you receive on the job that could result in your receiving more pay than the actual value of the services you performed. We deduct the value of subsidies and special conditions from your earnings when we decide whether you are working at the SGA level.

The Ticket to Work and Self-Sufficiency Program—The Ticket Program provides a ticket to disabled beneficiaries to take to a certified provider of their choice for rehabilitation and employment services.

Trial Work Period (SSDI)—A period of nine months (not necessarily consecutive) during which the earnings of a Social Security beneficiary who is blind or disabled will not affect his or her benefit. (The nine months of work must occur within a 60-month period).☺

The thing always happens that you really believe in; and the belief in a thing makes it happen.

FRANK LOYD WRIGHT

CHAPTER 10

SURVIVING ON YOUR WITS

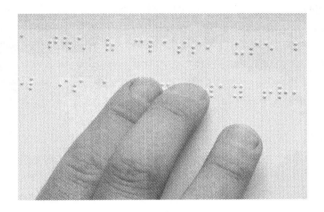

Unless you have some capacity to work or someone else to subsidize your disability income, just sitting around waiting for your check month-to-month, is a sure way to starve in the future. Create a new job or business from your knowledge, abilities, skills and opportunities (KASOs). Many disabled adults have some KASOs (expertise) in what interests them. For example, if you were a bookkeeper, you might choose to offer a service about resource scheduling or time and billing. Whatever your level of expertise professional or hobbyist—you can create a new career or business that shares your knowledge with others— and one that will succeed in a recession.

Create an opportunity for yourself where none seem to exist. Find a need and fill it. Once you think about it, you will know how to fill those needs. Some of the main elements that will make you successful is to learn business creativity, how to be an entrepreneur and how to market your service or enlist a specialist to promote your work. This expense can be incorporated in your PASS.

In fact, you are actually the ideal person to market your own business and will do better than a professional, simply because you know your business best. And because both your funds and time are limited when you are first starting out, you will probably have to rely more heavily on creativity than someone who has a degree in marketing and unlimited funds. And in marketing any small business, it is creativity that counts. A standard way to begin is to plan your service. Start with a simple outline that contains the description of what you want to achieve, and perhaps, since you are an expert, a brief bio that explains how you gained your expertise.

If you are considering submitting a PASS application with a work goal of self-employment, you must include a detailed business plan. This is the format I used to get over $15,000 (that does not have to be repaid) to start a business. Your business plan must include the following components to strengthen it:

I.   **Statement of Purpose**
       A. Name and Address of Business
       B. Nature of the Business
       C. Management Team
       D. Financing Required
       E. Statement of Confidentiality

II.   **Products or Services**
       A. Size of Business
       B. Legal Structure of Business
       C. Brief Discussion of Management
       D. History of the Business (date started, etc.)

III. Marketing Analysis

    A. Industry Analysis (current size of market)

    B. Industry Forecasts (future trends and outlook)

    C. Market Segmentation

IV. Marketing Plan

    A. Pricing

    B. Promotional Strategy

    C. Marketing Budget

    D. Analysis of Competition

V. Operation Plan

    A. Production Plan

    B. Distribution

    C. Location of Facilities

    D. Personnel

    E. Management (roles, duties and background)

    F. Management Support

VI. Contingency Plan [You will need to ask yourself and answer the following questions]

    A. Handling Major Problems?

    B. How changing health conditions would impact your business or work?

    C. What if you are unable to work due to your medications regimen in terms of its ever changing side effects; will you be able to meet your net income targets under these new conditions?

    D. What if you are unable to continue with your PASS?

    E. What if you have five customers scheduled Monday through Friday; how will you avoid a scheduling conflict and overbooking yourself?

    F. The risk of running out of cash?

    G. A drop in sales or insufficient sales?

H. Do you have adequate personal assistance? Will you be able to receive assistance at your job?

I. Are you prepared for emergencies? Do you have difficulty moving about or communicating? If there is an emergency, will your employers be able to provide you with assistance?

J. Have you considered all of your transportation needs? Will you use public transportation or purchase a vehicle?

K. Dishonesty, theft, and supply shrinkage?

L. Business Recessions?

M. Marketing Challenges?

VII.   Financial Plan

A. Cash Flow Projections

B. Income Statement Projections

C. Balance Sheets (pro-forma or current)

D. Breakeven Analysis

VIII.   Assessment Risk

A. Financing Being Requested

B. Equity Injection

C. Sources and Uses of Funds

IX.   Executive Summary

X.   Appendices and Supporting Documents

Pay special attention to section VI. Contingency Plan which is a key component SSA will look for before approving your PASS. The second most important section is section VII. Financial Plan and Sources and Uses of Funds. After your plan is completed and submitted to the PASS Cadre for review, you may be informed that your plan requires a feasibility study from the Small

Business Administration or Small Business Development Center to concur that you have the ability to start and operate your business successfully.

Helpful Tip: Be prepared to discuss and explain your business plan.

If you are considering employment, perhaps you can sell your services better by being employed as a corporation which you can set up to do the job, hence a PASS consultant. You do the work, but are employed by your corporation. Your own KASOs are the keys to establishing your new career—you are the expert.☺

CHAPTER 11

SELF EMPLOYMENT REQUIRED DOCUMENTS FOR SOLE PROPRIETOR

Many self-employed borrowers prefer to use home mortgage programs that will allow them to use their bank statements for income documentation to qualify for a mortgage loan. Usually, the total deposits of these bank statements will be added up each month and then divided by the required total number of months being used. Then the monthly average will be used as the monthly income for qualifying for the loan. The following documents that could be required by lenders:

- 12 months of bank statements
- Sole Proprietor—Schedule C—Personal Tax Return
- Copies of your Federal income tax returns for the past two years including all schedules

Most recent year-to-date profit and loss statement signed and dated by your accountant.☺

Ambition, confidence, enthusiasm and success are produced by courage, faith, pride and hard work.

HARRY F. BANKS

CHAPTER 12

MY PASS SUCCESS STORY

The vehicle that SSA bought for my business

I worked for 30 years before disability and had to depend on SSDI and Medicare health coverage for which I am neither proud nor ashamed. I used a PASS to set aside SSDI and earnings, which allowed me to purchase the car in the photo for my business. The PASS also allowed me to qualify for SSI and Medicaid.

My goal was to become self-reliant through entrepreneurship. However, I did not have a clue about how I would get startup funds needed for my proposed home based business. Nevertheless, by faith in God, I was already preparing my business plan. When I discovered PASS, I developed a stronger determination to achieve my occupational goal, which meant extensive research and due diligence to make my dream come true.

Obtaining a PASS was a very challenging yet worthy achievement. I had to prove my ability to manage a business and that the PASS was appropriate for me. Unfortunately, vocational rehab denied me services; but fortunately, SSA approved my PASS for over $16,000 to start and operate my business for 21 months.

As a self-advocate and self-vocational rehabilitation counselor, I determined what was necessary to start my home based business, i.e. personal computer, supplies, cell phone, accounting assistance, vehicle, etc. After launching the business and one year of saving, I purchased a very reliable, used vehicle. My PASS success allowed me to receive full SSI and full SSDI to accomplish my work goal.

Hope deferred maketh the heart sick; but when the desire cometh, it is a tree of life. Proverbs 13:12

This is the AFTER picture of my inexpensive, fixer-upper house purchased for $20,000 and renovated inside and out with home rehabilitation grants, as a person with disabilities. Initially, I paid $1,000 down in two payments for a 5-year mortgage (land deed) at 8% interest, $381 per month, until I could get traditional financing. After repairing my credit and attending a first-time homebuyer's course, I refinanced the house to obtain a proper deed. My final monthly mortgage payment was $219.00.

This is the BEFORE picture. Because my house was located in an Empowerment Zone (blighted area); and my disability, the yearly property taxes were $18.00. I received a grant for home weatherization assistance which provided custom insulated windows and front door, whole-house insulation and energy efficient wall-mounted heaters; a home improvement grant which provided a new porch and a home maintenance grant which provided plumbing, kitchen floor construction, new flooring and roof repair. I also received an energy assistance grant that paid my past due home energy bill.☺

Success consists of a series of little daily victories.

LADDIE F. HUTAR

CHAPTER 13

PASS KIT

These sample forms are provided to help you apply for a PASS and keep the records you will need to follow it. These are how-to materials to write your own PASS you will not find anywhere else. If your PASS is approved, remember to keep all your PASS papers in chronological order. Buy a notebook and tape every receipt to a page. Write the date of purchase and any other information you might need later, to explain that particular expense or income.

Keep a chronological record of all your phone contacts with SSA: date, time, purpose of the call, any information you received or gave out and the name of the person you spoke to. I wish you great success!☺

SAMPLE COMPLETED PLAN FOR ACHIEVING SELF-SUFFICIENCY (PASS)

(Simply customize the PASS below by filling in your own information rather than fake name and information)

In order to minimize recontacts or processing delays, please complete all questions and provide thorough explanations where requested. If you need additional space to answer any questions, use the Remarks section or a separate sheet of paper.

Date Received

Name   SSN

PART 1 – YOUR WORK GOAL
A. What is your work goal? *(Show the specific job you expect to have at the end of the plan. If you do not yet have a specific work goal and will be working with a vocational professional to find a suitable job match, show "VR Evaluation." If you show "VR Evaluation," be sure to complete Part II, question F on page 4.)*

My work goal is to become an Office Assistant. I enjoy duties related to the title of Office Clerk such as: counts, weighs, or measures material. Sorts and files records. Stuffs envelopes by hand or with envelope stuffing machine. Conveys messages, and runs errands. Stamps, sorts, and distributes mail. Stamps or numbers forms by hand or machine. Photocopies documents using photocopier. Place cards, forms or other material in storage receptacle such as file cabinet, drawer, or box. Files correspondence, cards, invoices, receipts, and other records in designated or adapted system.

If your goal involves supported employment, show the number of hours of job coaching you will receive when you begin working (**N/A**) per week/month *(circle one)* **N/A**

Show the numbers of hours of job coaching you expect to receive after the plan is completed (**N/A**) per week/month *(circle one).*

B. Describe the duties you expect to perform in this job. Be as specific as possible *(standing, walking, sitting, lifting, stooping, bending, contact with the public, writing reports/documents, etc.)*

As described above.

C. How did you decide on this work goal and what makes this job attractive to you?

How do you expect to find a job by the time your plan is completed?
Any State University Career Counseling & Job Placement Vocational Rehabilitation Services. Networking through Personal & Professional relationships. School to Work Program

D. If your work goal does not involve self-employment, how much do you expect to earn each month (gross) after your plan is completed? (**N/A**)/month **$0/month**

E. If your work goal involves self-employment; explain why working for yourself will make you more self-supporting than working for someone else.

My Goal Does not involve Self-Employment

NOTE: If you plan to start your own business, attach a detailed business plan. At a minimum, the business plan must include the type of business; products or services to be offered by your business; a description of the market for the business; the advertising plan; technical assistance needed; tools, supplies, and equipment needed; and a profit-and-loss projection for the duration of the PASS and at least one year beyond its completion. Also include a description of how you intend to make this business succeed.

F. Did someone help you prepare this plan? (**X)$YES** $NO If "No," skip to G.

If "YES," show the name, address and telephone number of that individual or organization

Rehab Counselor, Honolulu Vocational Rehabilitation Services, Honolulu, Hawaii 00000, (XXX)-111-0000

May we contact them if we need additional information about your plan? (**X)$YES** $NO

Do you want us to send them a copy of our decision on your plan? (**X)$YES** $NO

Are they charging you a fee for this service? $YES (**X)$NO**

If "YES," how much are they charging?

G. Have you ever submitted a Plan for Achieving Self Support (PASS) to Social Security? (**X)$YES** (X)$NO If "NO," skip to Part II.

If "YES," complete the following:

Was a PASS ever approved for you? **$YES** $NO If "NO," skip to Part II.

If "YES," complete the following:

When was your most recent plan approved (month/year)? **07/28/98**

What was your work goal in that plan? **Vocational Evaluation through Community Work Experiences**

Did you complete that PASS? $YES **$NO**

If "NO," why weren't you able to complete it? **PASS not written for specific work goal.**

If "YES," why weren't you able to become self-supporting?

Why do you believe that this new plan you are requesting will help you go to work? **I have been able to identify an employment consultant willing to provide services in my community. It has been difficult to find an employment consultant able to provide liaison services with my school and community. I continue to have a strong support group, comprised of family, friends and school staff.**

PART II – MEDICAL/VOCATIONAL BACKGROUND

A. What are your disabling illnesses, injuries, or conditions?

My primary disability is Cerebral Palsy.

B. Describe any limitations you have because of your disability (e.g., limited amount of standing or lifting, stooping, bending, or walking; difficulty concentrating; unable to work with other people, difficulty handling stress, etc.) Be specific.

I will use a wheelchair to get around my employment settings. I will need to do seated work, will not be able to lift heavy objects, and will need adaptations to reach items above my head. I will need more time to learn the job initially and may perform the job at a slower rate than my co-workers.

In light of the limitations you described, how will you carry out the duties of your work goal?

C. List the jobs you have had **most often** in the past few years. Also list any jobs, including volunteer work, which are similar to your work goal or which provided you with skills that may help you perform the work goal. List the dates you worked in these jobs. Identify periods of self-employment. If you were in the Army, list your Military Occupational Specialty (MOS) code; for the Air Force, list your Air Force Specialty (AFSC) code; and for the Navy, Marine Corps, and Coast Guard, list your RATE.

Job Title Type of Business Dates Worked From To

Please refer to Remarks Section -- Summary of Work Experiences

D. Circle the highest grade of school completed. 0 1 2 3 4 5 6 7 8 9 10 11 12 (X)GED or High School Equivalency College: 1 **2** 3 4 or more 1. Were you awarded a college or postgraduate degree? $YES **$NO** If "NO," skip to 2. When did you graduate? What type of degree did you receive? (B.A., B.S., M.B.A., etc.) In what field of study? 2. Did you attend special education classes? $YES **(X)$NO** If "NO," skip to E. If "YES," complete the following:

Name of school Address: _____

Dates attended: From _____ To_____

Type of program _____

E. Have you completed any type of special job training, trade or vocational school?

(X)$YES (X)$NO If "NO," skip to F. If "YES," complete the following:

Type of training: **The skills I have acquired through my informal jobs at school, and will be useful in a paid job situation are: following directions, navigating independently around the school, working independently for an extended time and organizing items.**

Date completed:

Type of training:

Date completed:

Did you receive a certificate or license? X$YES **X$NO** If "NO," skip to F. If "YES," what kind of certificate or license did you receive?

F. Have you ever had or expect to have a vocational evaluation or an Individualized Written Rehabilitation Plan (IWRP) or an Individualized Employment Plan (IEP)? (X)$YES **(X)$NO** If "NO," skip to Part III (page 5). If "YES," attach a copy of the evaluation and skip to Part II (page 5). If you cannot attach a copy, complete the following:

When were you evaluated or when do you expect to be evaluated or when was the IWRP or IEP done or when do you expect it to be done? Show the name, address, and phone number of the person or organization who evaluated you or will evaluate you or who prepared the IWRP or IEP or will prepare the IWRP or IEP.

PART III – YOUR PLAN

I want my Plan to begin (month/year) and my Plan to end (month/year).

List the steps, in sequence that you will take to reach this work goal. Be as specific as possible. If you will be attending school, show the courses you will study each quarter/semester. Include the final steps to find a job once you have obtained the tools, education, services, etc., that you need.

Past Steps (Accomplishments to Date)
Performed Job Trial at Local Grocery Store. On 04/22/98.
Transition planning including employment as part of IEP. From 05/98 to 05/2002.
PASS Submitted 5/98 for approval to SSA.
PASS Approved 07/28/98.
Funds released for PASS 10/98.
Performed school-based Job trials: From 09/98 to 04/99.
Performed Job Trial at Local Market
Performed Job Trial at Grocery Store
Perform on the job training at Local Market. During 04/99.
Perform on the job training at Pizza Restaurant. During 04/99.
Perform on the job training at Shirt Store. During 03/99.
Identify evaluator to complete Vocational Profile. From 10/98 to 11/98.

Steps Upon Approval of PASS Plan
Continue community-based Job Trials: From 11/98 to 06/99
Continue to Gather additional assessment information. From 12/98 to 09/99.
Complete written Vocational Profile Document. From 02/99 to 09/99.
Hold Profile Meeting and Identify specific employers to contact re: hiring John Doe. From 03/99 to 09/99.
Revise and Extend PASS to incorporate my vocational goal derived from the Vocational Evaluation as required. From 04/99 to 06/99.
Obtain estimates on van. From 04/99 to 06/99.
Submit this PASS Plan. During 06/99.
Receive retroactive PASS funds for Van down-payment. From 06/99 to 07/99.
Purchase accessible van. From 06/99 to 08/99.
Research and purchase auto insurance. From 04/99 to 08/99.
Set up a maintenance schedule for van. From 08/99 to 06/2001.
Incorporate related curriculum in the Individual Education Plan (IEP). From 09/99 to 06/2003.
Structure classes in related employment area. From 09/99 to 06/2003.
Participate in School to Work Program. From 09/2001 to 06/2003.
Continue Life Skills Training and work with OT, PT, and Speech Therapists. From 06/99 to 06/2003. Develop multiple long-term jobs working with local employers and IEP curriculum for School To Work employment .From 09/99 to 06/2003.

Continue on-going tutoring throughout school year and summers.

Obtain part time clerical support position-15-20 hours/week during school summers and increasing to 30-35 hours/week after graduation from high school. From 06/99 to 06/2003.

Received On The Job Training
From 06/2002 to 06/2003.
Job Coaching during high school and summers will consist of one-on-one supports, decreasing and increasing as job duties are expanded and will be decreased to one to two hours/week after high school Graduation.

Apply for ST Vocational Rehabilitation Services
From 09/2000 to 10/2000

Complete PASS Requirements

As of 06/2001

PART IV – EXPENSES

A. If you propose to purchase, lease, or rent a vehicle, please provide the following additional information:

1. Explain why less expensive forms of transportation *(e.g., public transportation, cabs)* will not allow you to reach your work goal.

2. Do you currently have a valid driver's license? (X)$YES **(X)$NO** If "YES," skip to 3. If "NO," complete the following: **My disability will not allow me to attain a driver's license. I plan to contract with family members to perform this service.**

Does Part III include the steps you will follow to get a driver's license? $YES **$NO**

If "YES," skip to 3. If "NO," complete the following:

Who will drive the vehicle? **My family and I live 21+ miles from the nearest town of # population. The nearest community with increased vocational opportunities is 45+ miles away. Public forms of transportation are not available to me. It is not reasonable to request assistance from neighbors due to inconvenience and my transportation needs.**

How will it be used to help you with your work goal?

3. If you are proposing to **purchase** a vehicle, explain why renting or leasing are not sufficient. **Because of special accommodations. My family and I have not been able to find a used van that will adapt to our needs.**

4. Explain why you chose the particular vehicle. (**Note**: the purchase of the vehicle should be listed as one of the steps in Part III.) **Low mileage, adaptable used conversion vans are difficult to find. It may cost more to adapt a used vehicle to my needs.**

B. If you propose to purchase computer equipment or other expensive equipment, please explain why a less expensive alternative (e.g., rental of a computer or purchase of a less expensive model) will not allow you to reach your goal. Explain why you need the capabilities of the particular computer/equipment you identified. Also, if you attend (or will attend) a school with a computer lab for student use, explain why use of that facility is not sufficient to meet your needs.

1. Item/service: **Job Development and On-the-Job Training. Cost: $10,000.00**
Vendor/provider: **J. J. and Future Contracted Supports**
Why needed: **To assist me to secure a paid job and establish necessary supports to learn, perform, and maintain the job.**
How will you pay for this item (e.g., one-time payment, monthly payment)? **No Cost to PASS Plan. ST Vocational Rehabilitation and Any Town Schools will be responsible.**
How did you determine the cost? **Estimate of 200 needed hours at $50/hour.**

2. Item/service: **Van Cost: $12,000.00**
Vendor/provider: **Local Chevrolet Dealer with local Surgical Supply**
Why needed: **Provide safe transportation to work.**
How will you pay for this item (e.g., one-time payment, monthly payment)? **Monthly payments**
How did you determine the cost? **Received two estimates and made determination on the package best suited to my needs. I have decided to use a company from this area to ensure available service. An out of state company may be cheaper at time of purchase but will not be able to provide me with needed service without having to travel great distances. The cost of shipping the conversion and other additions was also considered. Payments for a five-year period will be approximately $790.00. Maintenance will be low as the van and equipment will be under warranty. I will be sharing the cost of the van with my brother Louis whom is also developing a PASS. The total van cost with all modifications is $35,000.00**

3. Item/service: **Van Insurance Cost: $100.00/month**
Vendor/provider: **Local Insurance**
Why needed: **Insurance required by state law and bank requirement**
How will you pay for this item (e.g., one-time payment, monthly payment)? **Quarterly**
How did you determine the cost? **Phone Estimate**
Insurance Costs will not be charged to the PASS Plan -- will be responsibility of family.

4. Item/service: **Operational Costs, Gas, Maintenance and Tags Cost: $90.00/month**
Vendor/provider: **Local Service Stations**
Why needed: **Vehicle Maintenance to and from work**
How will you pay for this item (e.g., one-time payment, monthly payment)? **Weekly**
How did you determine the cost? **Estimated rural distances to employers. Costs will not be charged to the PASS Plan -- will be responsibility of family.**

C. Other than the items identified in A or B above, list the items or services you are buying or renting or will need to buy or rent in order to reach your work goal. Be as specific as possible. If schooling is an item, list tuition, fees, books, etc. as separate items. List the cost for the entire length of time you will be in school. Where applicable, include brand and model number of the item. **(Do not include expenses you were paying prior to the beginning of your plan; only additional expenses incurred because of your plan can be approved.)**

NOTE: Be sure that Part III shows when you will purchase these items or services or training.

1. Item/service: **Job Development and On-the-Job Training. Cost: $10,000.00**
Vendor/provider: **J. J. and Future Contracted Supports**
Why needed: **To assist me to secure a paid job and establish necessary supports to learn, perform, and maintain the job.**
How will you pay for this item (e.g., one-time payment, monthly payment)? **No Cost to PASS Plan. ST Vocational Rehabilitation and Any Town Schools will be responsible.**
How did you determine the cost? **Estimate of 200 needed hours at $50/hour.**

2. Item/service: **Van Cost: $12,000.00**
Vendor/provider: **Local Chevrolet Dealer with local Surgical Supply**
Why needed: **Provide safe transportation to work.**
How will you pay for this item (e.g., one-time payment, monthly payment)? **Monthly payments**
How did you determine the cost? **Received two estimates and made determination on the package best suited to my needs. I have decided to use a company from this area to ensure available service. An out of state company may be cheaper at time of purchase but will not be able to provide me with needed service without having to travel great distances. The cost of shipping the conversion and other additions was also considered. Payments for a five-year period will be approximately $790.00. Maintenance will be low as the van and equipment will be under warranty. I will be sharing the cost of the van with my brother Louis whom is also developing a PASS. The total van cost with all modifications is $35,000.00**

3. Item/service: **Van Insurance Cost: $100.00/month**
Vendor/provider: **Local Insurance**
Why needed: **Insurance required by state law and bank requirement**
How will you pay for this item (e.g., one-time payment, monthly payment)?
Quarterly
How did you determine the cost? **Phone Estimate**
Insurance Costs will not be charged to the PASS Plan -- will be responsibility of family.

4. Item/service: **Operational Costs, Gas, Maintenance and Tags Cost: $90.00/month**
Vendor/provider: **Local Service Stations**
Why needed: **Vehicle Maintenance to and from work**
How will you pay for this item (e.g., one-time payment, monthly payment)?
Weekly
How did you determine the cost? **Estimated rural distances to employers. Costs will not be charged to the PASS Plan -- will be responsibility of family.**

D. If you indicated in Part II (page 4) that you have a college degree or specialized training, and your plan includes additional education or training, explain why the education/training you already received is not sufficient to allow you to be self-supporting. **N/A.**

E. What are your current expenses each month *(rent, food, utilities, phone, property taxes, homeowner's insurance automobile repair and maintenance, public transportation costs, clothes, laundry/dry cleaning, charity contributions, etc.)?*

If the amount of income you will have available for living expenses after making payments or saving money for your plan expenses is **less than** your current living expenses, explain how you will pay for your living expenses. **N/A.**

PART V – FUNDING FOR WORK GOAL

A. Do you plan to use any items you already own (e.g., equipment or property) to reach your work goal? **X$YES** $NO If "NO," skip to B. If "YES," complete the following: **1. Wheelchair, for mobility and access to employment, Value = $1,800.00**

B. Have you saved any money to pay for the expenses listed on pages 6-8 in Part IV? *(Include cash on hand or money in a bank account.)* *(X)*$YES (X)$NO If "NO," skip to C. If "YES," how much have you saved?)? **$2768.00 saved in a bank account.**

D. Do you receive or expect to receive income other than SSI payments? **(X)$YES** $NO If "NO," skip to F. If "YES," provide details as follows: **Type of Income Amount Frequency** *(Weekly, Monthly, Yearly)* **$250.00 Adoption subsidy. +$148.00 Survivor's Benefits**

E. How much of this income will you use each month to pay for the expenses listed in Part IV? **$398.00/month**

F. Do you plan to save any or all of this money for a future purchase which is necessary to complete your goal? **X$YES** $ NO If "NO," skip to F. If "YES," how will you keep the money separate from other money you have? *(If you will keep the savings in a separate bank account, give the name and address of the bank and the account number.)* **Local State Bank, XXX Street, Any Town, Any State, 00000.**

G. Will any other person or organization (e.g., Vocational Rehabilitation, school grants, Job Partnership Training Assistance (JPTA) pay for or reimburse you for any part of the expenses listed in Part IV or provide any other items or services you will need? **(X)$YES** (X)$NO If "NO," skip to Part VI. If "YES," provide details as follows:

Who Will Pay Item/service? **Vocational Rehab, Van Lift for $ 5,500 as of 9/1999. JTPA Support, Conversion Package for $10,510 as of 9/1999. Institute on Disabilities, PASS Consult for $ 2,500 as of 6/1999. United Cerebral Palsy, Vocational Services for $14,000 as of 9/1999.**

Amount?
When will the item/service be purchased?

PART VI- REMARKS

By Coordinator, on behalf of John Doe.
In the job trials John Doe has participated in he has exhibited a strong work ethic. He especially enjoys tasks and environments that are new. He is not distracted by new environments and working with unfamiliar people. John Doe has a good attention to detail and has the capability to be a very meticulous worker if he likes what he is doing. His O.T. and aide witnessed his best performance when he is seated, due to lack of balance. John Doe is a compassionate young man. When he visits a local nursing home to volunteer, he attempts to communicate with residents in the halls and reaches out to touch their hands. John Doe is a social young man and likes interacting with people in general but seems to especially like spending time with older males. John Doe really enjoys being able to do things for himself. His interests include: computers, pets, jewelry, and physical activities like lifting weights.

John Doe uses a wheelchair and a walker to move throughout an environment. His stamina is good. He has a fantastic memory and can navigate through large buildings independently. Crag can transition into a vehicle by using his walker. John Doe's speech is sometimes difficult to understand even by people who know him well. He and his support staff are currently researching augmentative communication devices for more effective methods of communication. John Doe needs support in the event that he has a seizure. He does lose consciousness and may slide out of his wheelchair.

Job Trial Summaries:

Pizza Restaurant: John Doe washed tables. Although he followed a prescribed pattern for washing the tables he was not thorough enough to remove all food from the table. John Doe appeared bored with the task and seemed to dislike wearing the rubber gloves and putting his hands in the bleach water used to clean the tables. However, he did seem to enjoy cleaning pool tables. He was quite thorough removing all debris from the table, and again was able to follow a prescribed pattern for cleaning the table. He used a roller brush to perform the task.

Local Gym Training: John Doe performed a job trial assembling bicycle breaks as a consultant learner for training. During the 30-minute trial he worked with people whom he had never met before, in an unfamiliar place, performing an unfamiliar task. Several people whom he knew (his mom, brother, aide and teacher were in the room at the time of his trial but were not interacting with him). There were many other distractions in the room as well; three other consultant learners were also performing the task simultaneously and 20 people were participating in the training. John Doe remained focused on the task at hand. He had some difficulty performing some of the assembly steps which required fine motor coordination, e.g. picking up a break shoe by grasping it between the index finger and thumb. John Doe persisted through these steps attempting to perform the task independently. He was meticulous in performance of each step. His speed was slow but it was unclear if it was caused by his thoroughness or the difficulty with the fine motor requirements of the task.

Local Cafe: John Doe practiced rolling silverware at the Any Town Cafe for 1-2 hours. Although he was able to roll one utensil in a napkin, he was unable to roll all three pieces at a time and keep the napkin tight due to lack of dexterity. The business is small and congested; this made it difficult for John Doe to move around the business with his wheelchair. John Doe exhibits dulled sensitivity to temperatures; it may not be wise to employ John Doe in eating establishments where safety could be an issue.

Shirt Store: John Doe folded tee shirts for two hours. He was able to follow the prescribed steps shown to him by the owner. He folded the shirts neatly, smoothing out the wrinkles as he worked, and he sorted the shirts by color. John Doe's performance was better folding the smaller shirts than the larger shirts since he could reach all the sides of the smaller shirt. Accommodations would have made it easier to complete tasks efficiently in a sitting position.

Local Market and Grocery Store Chain: John Doe performed the task of facing shelves in both grocery stores. He was able to work independently for at least 30 minutes. John Doe organized the shelves neatly ensuring all labels faced forward and rotated merchandise. John Doe exhibited pride in his work at this site.

PART VII – AGREEMENT

If my plan is approved, I agree to:

☐   Comply with all of the terms and conditions of the plan as approved by the Social Security Administration (SSA);

☐   Report any changes in my plan **to SSA** immediately:

☐   Keep records and receipts of all expenditures I make under the plan until asked to provide them to SSA:

☐   Use the income or resources set aside under the plan **only** to buy the items or services shown in the plan as approved by SSA.

I realize that if I do not comply with the terms of the plan or if I use the income or resources set aside under my plan for any other purpose, SSA will count the income or resources that were excluded and I may have to repay the additional SSI I received.

I also realize that SSA may not approve any expenditures for which I do not submit receipts or other proof of payment.

I know that anyone who makes or causes to be made a false statement or representation of material fact in an application for use in determining a right to payment under the Social Security Act commits a crime punishable under Federal Law and/or State Law. I affirm that all the information I have given on this form is true.

Signature:_____
Date:
Address:
Home:
Work:

PRIVACY ACT STATEMENT

The Social Security Administration is allowed to collect the information on this form under section 1631(e) of the Social Security Act. We need this information to determine if we can approve your plan for achieving self-support.
Giving us this information is voluntary. However, without it, we may not be able to approve your plan. Social Security will not use the information for any other purpose.

We would give out the facts on this form without your consent only in certain situations. For example, we give out this information if a Federal law requires us to or if your congressional Representative or Senator needs the information to answer questions you ask them.

PAPERWORK REDUCTION ACT NOTICE AND TIME IT TAKES STATEMENT:

The **Paperwork Reduction Act of 1995** requires us to notify you that this information collection is in accordance with the clearance requirements of section 3507 of the Paperwork Reduction Act of 1995. We may not conduct or sponsor and you are not required to respond to, a collection of information unless it displays a valid OMB control number. We estimate that it will take you about 120 minutes to complete this form. This includes the time it will take to read the instructions, gather the necessary facts and fill out the form.

OUR RESPONSIBILITIES TO YOU

We received your plan for achieving self-support (PASS) on _____.

Your plan will be processed by Social Security employees who are trained to work with PASS.

The PASS expert handling your case will work directly with you. He or she will look over the plan as soon as possible to see if there is a good chance that you can meet your work goal. The PASS expert will also make sure that the things you want to pay for are needed to achieve your work goal and are reasonably priced. If changes are needed, the PASS expert will discuss them with you.

You may contact the PASS expert toll-free at 1-_____.

YOUR REPORTING AND RECORDKEEPING RESPONSIBILITIES

If we approve your plan, you must tell Social Security about any changes to your plan. You must tell us if:

$ Your medical condition improves.

$ You are unable to follow your plan.

$ You decide not to pursue your goal or decide to pursue a different goal.

$ You decide that you do not need to pay for any of the expenses you listed in your plan.

$ Someone else pays for any of your plan expenses.

$ You use the income or resources we exclude for a purpose other than the expenses specified in your plan.

$ There are any other changes to your plan.

You must tell us about any of these things within 10 days following the month in which it happens. If you do not report any of these things, we may stop your plan.

You should also tell us if you decide that you need to pay for other expenses not listed in your plan in order to reach your goal. We may be able to change your plan or the amount of income we exclude so you can pay for the additional expenses.

YOU MUST KEEP RECEIPTS OR CANCELLED CHECKS TO SHOW WHAT EXPENSES YOU PAID FOR AS PART OF THE PLAN. You need to keep these receipts or cancelled checks until we contact you to find out if you are still following your plan. When we contact you, we will ask to see the receipts or cancelled checks. If you are not following the plan, you man have to pay back some or all of the SSI you received.

(Download this form at http://www.ssa.gov/online/ssa-545.html)

SAMPLE PASS GOALS AND MILESTONES FORMAT

(This is the format I used, change it as you prefer)

Goals Statement		
Work Goal Support	Beginning Date	Completion Date
Office Equipment and Supplies		
Supplies and Equipment		
Major Operational Tasks		
Bookkeeping and Communications		
Promotions and Advertising		
Transportation		
PASS Completed and Goal Met		
Comment		

EXAMPLE PERSONAL BUDGET
Where Does Your Beneficiary Check Go?

[Your budget must be based on your living expenses in subsidized or other affordable housing]

Monthly Non-Business Income
Salary	0
Investment Income	0
SSDI	749
Other Income	0
Retirement Benefits	0
Less Taxes	0
Net Monthly Income	749
*Total Monthly SSDI Income	749

Monthly Non-Business Expenses
Rent/Mortgage	225
Utilities	0
Homeowner's Insurance	0
Property Taxes	0
Home Repairs	0
Groceries	165
Telephone	70
Tuition	0
Transportation	45
Child Care	0
Medical Expenses	0
Clothing, Laundry, Personal Items	
Insurance Premiums:	0
Life, Disability, Auto, Medical	0
Miscellaneous:	
Entertainment, Vacation,	
Gifts, Dues, Fees, etc.	0
Auto Loans	0
Consumer Debt	0
**Total Monthly Expenses	505
Monthly Surplus/Deficit:	
(Income Minus Expenses)	244<+>

*Total Monthly Income to be set aside monthly minus $20
**Total Monthly Expenses must not exceed impending SSI benefits

DISABILITY EMPOWERMENT

NON-DISCLOSURE/NON-COMPETE AGREEMENT
DURING INITIAL START-UP PHASE

I, _____ (Full Name), have been invited to review this information that has been gathered at considerable expenses to others and has been shared with me due to my possible involvement. I agree not to share or use this information (Name of Company or Reviewer), or use it for myself to enter into a competitive venture.

_____
(Business Plan Owner's Signature)

_____
(Company or Reviewer's Signature)

SAMPLE COVER LETTER
FROM APPLICANT WITH DISABILITY

[You should use this letter as an opportunity to explain in your own words; how the PASS is expected to help you become self-sufficient. Simply customize the letter below by filling in your own information rather than fake name and other information.]

{ADDRESS}
{DATE}
{PASS CADRE SPECIALIST NAME/ADDRESS}

Dear {Mr. or Ms.}

In response to your letter dated XXXXXXXX, enclosed please find the following documents in support of (Your Name) application for the approval of a Plan for Achieving Self Support (PASS):

- Social Security Letters
- Completed PASS application (Form SSA-545-BK) with more details in Part III.
- Business Plan with Supporting Documents
- Feasibility Evaluation from the Small Business Development Center

Jane Doe plans to use his or her PASS to XXXX.

Sincerely,

XXXX
Jane Doe

Enclosures (4)

SAMPLE LETTER FROM REHABILITATION COUNSELOR

[Simply customize the letter below by filling in your own information rather than fake name and other information.]

{ADDRESS}
{DATE}
{PASS CADRE SPECIALIST NAME/ADDRESS}

Dear {Mr. or Ms.}

I am writing on behalf of John Doe, a 30-year-old male. Please accept this letter as support for Mr. Doe's Plan for Achieving Self Support (PASS).

I am employed by the Hawaii Department of Labor, Rehabilitation Services, Vocational Rehabilitation Program (VRP) and have been Mr. Doe's rehabilitation counselor since July 2006. VRP has agreed to sponsor Mr. Doe through an approved Individual Written Rehabilitation Plan (IWRP) with a goal of Elementary Education Teacher. I am fully familiar with Mr. Doe's academic record and with the extent of his disability and fully support his goal of becoming a teacher.

Under VRP, IWRP we will provide Mr. Doe with funding for the following:

- Four years of college tuition at $1,700 per semester
- Van modifications at a cost of $14,000
- Transportation to and from the Honolulu University campus by private carrier
- A per semester allotment for books. A laptop computer to use in his studies

VRP fully supports Mr. Doe's need for his own vehicle. Since many teaching openings occur in the outlying suburbs and small towns, where there is not public transportation available, having his own van makes it more likely that he will find work.

We also support Mr. Doe's need to purchase a new van. Based on VRP's experience, we discourage our consumers from purchasing used vehicles if they are to be equipped with hydraulic lifts and other modifications for the wheelchair user. We have found that there are fewer problems if these modifications are installed on a new vehicle. Also, in a case like Mr. Doe's where he will need $14,000 worth of modifications, VRP's policy is that we will not pay for modifications if they exceed the fair market value of the vehicle. Please call me at 000-0000 if you have any questions.

Sincerely,

XXXX
Rehab Counselor

Enclosures (4)

SAMPLE LETTER FROM ADVOCATE

[Simply customize the letter below by filling in your own information rather than fake name and other information.]

{ADDRESS}
{DATE}
{PASS CADRE SPECIALIST NAME/ADDRESS}

Dear {Mr. or Ms.}

This office represents John Doe. Enclosed please find the following documents in support of his Plan for Achieving Self Sufficiency (PASS):

- Completed PASS application (form SSA-545-BK)
- Letter of John Doe, PASS applicant
- Invoice showing current price of Dodge Caravan
- Provisional letter of acceptance form Honolulu University
- Letter from XXXX Rehab Counselor, Office of Vocational and Educational Services for Individuals with Disabilities

Mr. Doe plans to use his PASS to save for the full purchase price of a Dodge Caravan which he will purchase in July 2007. Although the Program Operations Manual System (POMS) has a general rule limiting PASS expenditures for vehicles to the down payment, Mr. Doe falls within an exception to that rule. (See POMS SI E00870.006E.3.c., providing that the down payment can be the full cost of the item if no monthly payment would be financially manageable.) As Mr. Doe explains in his letter, he would be unable to meet his monthly living expenses and make monthly payments for the van out of the $749 he receives in Social Security payments if he purchased the van sooner than July 2007 by making a down payment and taking out an installment loan.

I believe the proposed PASS, as written, should be approved under current POMS criteria. Please do not hesitate to call me at 000-0000 with any questions.

Sincerely,

XXXX
Advocate

Enclosures (5)

SAMPLE PROPOSED SOURCES
AND START-UP USES OF FUNDS

Sources:
    SS PASS   15000
    Total Sources of Funds   <u>15000</u>

Uses:
Performing Service Tasks:
    Used Light Cargo Van or Pickup Truck   9000
    Commercial Automobile Insurance   690
Gas, Maintenance, Auto Rental (1 year)   808
Tag and Title   250
    Equipment and Supplies   250

Bookkeeping, Desktop Publishing, Communications:
    Computer   500
        HP Compaq Business Desktop dx2000
        Ideal for budget conscious users and
        Everyday office applications
    All-In-One Color Printer, Copier, Facsimile, Scanner
    Brother MFC-420CN   130
    Cell Phone   100
    Phone Card (1 year)   240
    Quicken Accounting Software   100
    Office Supplies   100

Operations:
    Reserve Business Name   80
Business License   125
Dishonesty Bond Insurance   234
General Liability Insurance   858
    Postage/PO Box   75
    Technical Assistance/Professional Fees   200

Promotional Materials and Advertising:
    Flyers, Business Cards, Card Stock   100
Advertising   1160
Publications, Leased Web Site/Hosting,
Magnetic Signage
    Subtotal Uses of Funds   <u>15000</u>

Total Funds Needed   15000

SAMPLE PASS EXPENSE ACCOUNTING FORM

[This is an actual form provided in the PASS reporting package. It will record the expenses as you pay them. Remember; always pay PASS expenses with a check to develop a proper "paper trail." Log in each check as you pay it. Be sure to include all your income, from whatever source. Save any W-2s you get from employers, and Notices of Award from SSA.]

Name/SSN

Month/Year:

I. **PASS Savings**

Amount deposited in PASS Account:

Income deposited in PASS Account:

Account Balance at End of Month:

II. **PASS Expenses**

Expense	Date Purchased	Amount
TOTAL:		

PLEASE ATTACH RECEIPTS AND BANK STATEMENTS

INCOME LOG

MONTH_____YEAR_____

AMOUNT	CHECK NUMBER	SOURCE	DATE
TOTALS:			

MEDICAL EXPENSES LOG

MONTH_____YEAR_____

AMOUNT	CHECK NUMBER	EXPENSE	DATE

I have learned that success is to be measured not so much by the position that one has reached in life as by the obstacles which he has overcome while trying to succeed.

BOOKER T. WASHINGTON

CHAPTER 14

THE AMERICAN DREAM FOR DISABLED AMERICANS: BE IT EVER SO SMALL AND CHEAP

Do not waste money on housing. You can buy a house cheaper than renting. $700 a month rent equals $16,800 in two years to the landlord.

Why make him rich? In houses, the good deal is the two or three-bedroom, one-bathroom mid-1950s bungalow or ranch. It is usually frame construction. Brick veneer is more costly, but holds its value. There are great quantities of good houses in low-cost areas of the country for $75,000 or less.

These houses often have wasted space in the attic (for extra bedrooms, etc.) and real rocking chair porches for wheelchair accessibility. Good owners are caretakers who love these houses and are constantly making repairs. To avoid a mortgage, you can sell your current house (if you already own one) to buy a smaller house then, live debt free! Small houses with two or three bedrooms are also found in older, blighted communities in the city that are no longer in decline, on the outskirts of town or in the country.

Most people not disabled prefer large, expensive, new homes. Let us disabled people follow the example of Warren Buffett, the billionaire, who still owns the house he bought in the mid-1950s for around $31,000.☺

...why be an average person? All the great achievements of history have been made by strong individuals who refused to consult statistics or to listen to those who could prove convincingly that what they wanted to do, and in fact ultimately did do, was completely impossible.

ERIC BUTTERWORTH

CHAPTER 15

BEATING SELF-DEFEAT

A highly effective way to beat back feelings of self-defeat is to know "it is possible." When facing a major crisis, too many disabled people give up prematurely because they are convinced "it is impossible."

However, those who overcome great trials do so because of their strong conviction that "it is possible." In the presence of a great personal trial or when dealing with a serious professional setback, build up positive affirmations such as these:

- It is possible for me to find a solution where none is apparent.
- It is possible for me to create a path where one does not now exist.
- It is possible for me to discover a breakthrough.
- It is possible for me to explore every alternative.
- It is possible for me to find people who can help.
- It is possible for me to respond with creativity and energy. ☺

When you feel like giving up, remember why you held on for so long in the first place.

UNKNOWN

CONTACT THE AUTHORESS

Tonza would like to hear about your success in obtaining your work goal or homeownership, using the PASS or alternative resources.

Tonza Borden
P.O. Box 115579
Atlanta, Georgia 30310

Courage is doing what you're afraid to do. There can be no courage unless you're scared.

EDDIE RICKENBACKER

SPECIAL BOOK REQUEST ORDER FORM

If you want to receive a spiral-bound version of **DISABILITY EMPOWERMENT** to your home address, through postal mail instead of you ordering the paperback or downloading on the internet. This is done by "SPECIAL REQUEST ONLY.

This complete printed version of **DISABILITY EMPOWERMENT** is an 8 ½ by 11, 112-page clear and concise instruction manual. It is shipped directly to you through the postal service by Tonza Borden (instead of downloading or trade paperback) and is done so by special customer request only and is non-refundable. In addition, with your purchase, you will receive FREE online consultation for 30 days, and Tonza Borden will personally answer any questions you may have in any areas of this book. I am sure you will find the information in this book to be of great use to you as it has been for others.

☐ Please RUSH **DISABILITY EMPOWERMENT** to:

Name: _____

Address: _____

City/State/Zip: _____

Book Cost: 14.95

SHIPPING AND HANDLING   3.05

TOTAL: **18.00**

Payment Method: ☐ Cash   ☐ Check   ☐ Money Order
         ☐ Pay Pal (tonzaborden@comcast.net)

Make checks and money orders payable to: **Tonza Borden**
Mail to: P.O. Box 115579
                                                                      Atlanta, GA 30310

Please allow 14 days for shipping.

*Checks are processed electronically – Check return fees apply for bounced checks

ABOUT THE AUTHORESS

Tonza Borden doesn't just write about disability. She is an author living with disability, on a mission to make a difference. She is the founder of Disability Empowerment Outreach Ministry, Inc. In between operating her business and her writing, she is passionately involved in the ministry of helps. Experiences as a disabled person fired her desire to help other people living with disabilities, which provide her an endless source of inspiration. Her ministry's *mission* is to provide resources and referrals to needy individuals facing challenges of disabilities and a crisis; and inspiration to achieve economic self-sufficiency.

Her ministry's *vision* is to encourage these individuals to seek ways to strengthen themselves physically, mentally and spiritually with the goal of becoming productive and contributing members of mainstream society. The organization will offer programs that help support and inspire disabled individuals who want to work.

Her ministry's *goals* are:

- Focus on improving disabled adults economic prospects;
- Deploy strategies aimed at improving their chances to earn a living that allows them to survive and thrive in their community; and
- Make referrals to community supports that they need in their daily lives.

The services and programs are carried out locally utilizing the best experts available to assist her.

You are not alone. Believe you can succeed and you will.

TONZA BORDEN

CPSIA information can be obtained
at www.ICGtesting.com
Printed in the USA
FSHW012010020521
81067FS